EASY FRENCH WORD GAMES & PUZZLES

WITHDRAWN

Maurie N. Taylor

PASSPORT BOOKS
a division of *NTC Publishing Group*
Lincolnwood, Illinois USA

NTC PUZZLE AND LANGUAGE GAME BOOKS

Multilingual Resources
Puzzles & Games in Language Teaching

Spanish
Classroom Games in Spanish
Spanish Crossword Puzzles
Spanish Verbs and Vocabulary Bingo Games
Spanish Culture Puzzles
Spanish Vocabulary Puzzles
Let's Play Games in Spanish, 1, 2

French
Jouez le jeu!
Let's Play Games in French
Classroom Games in French
French Crossword Puzzles
French Word Games
French Grammar Puzzles
French Verbs and Vocabulary Bingo Games
French Word Games for Beginners
French Culture Puzzles

German
German Crossword Puzzles
German Word Games for Beginners
Let's Play Games in German

Italian
Italian Crossword Puzzles

Japanese
Let's Play Games in Japanese

Chinese
Let's Play Games in Chinese

For further information or a current catalog, write:
National Textbook Company
a division of *NTC Publishing Group*
4255 West Touhy Avenue
Lincolnwood, Illinois 60646-1975 U.S.A.

1992 Printing

INTRODUCTION

Puzzles and word games offer a double advantage to all beginners in a foreign language: they are instructive as well as being fun. *Easy French Word Games & Puzzles* has been specially designed to test your knowledge of French vocabulary and spelling in ways that will both challenge and amuse you. And, as this book helps you learn, it may very well uncover a great deal of knowledge you never knew you had!

The 53 games in this collection include *anagrammes, catégogrilles, labyrinthes, croix de mots, motstractions, lettres en chiffres,* and *arcs-en-mots* that deal with specific areas of vocabulary, such as clothing, furniture, animals, and months of the year. Each puzzle format focuses on different aspects of your French spelling and word skills, while adding to the variety and enjoyment this book provides.

Work through this book by yourself or with others. Either way, *Easy French Word Games & Puzzles* will bring you hours of pleasure along with a great deal of valuable French-language experience. And remember, if you should have any difficulty with a puzzle clue, complete solutions have been provided for you at the back of the book.

EXEMPLES D' ANAGRAMMES

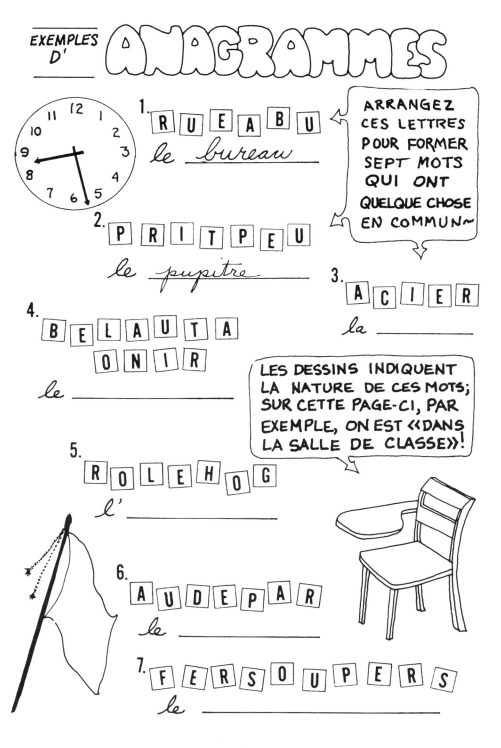

1. R U E A B U
le *bureau*

ARRANGEZ CES LETTRES POUR FORMER SEPT MOTS QUI ONT QUELQUE CHOSE EN COMMUN~

2. P R I T P E U
le *pupitre*

3. A C I E R
la _____

4. B E L A U T A O N I R
le _____

LES DESSINS INDIQUENT LA NATURE DE CES MOTS; SUR CETTE PAGE-CI, PAR EXEMPLE, ON EST «DANS LA SALLE DE CLASSE»!

5. R O L E H O G
l' _____

6. A U D E P A R
le _____

7. F E R S O U P E R S
le _____

ANAGRAMMES

VOIR PAGE 1

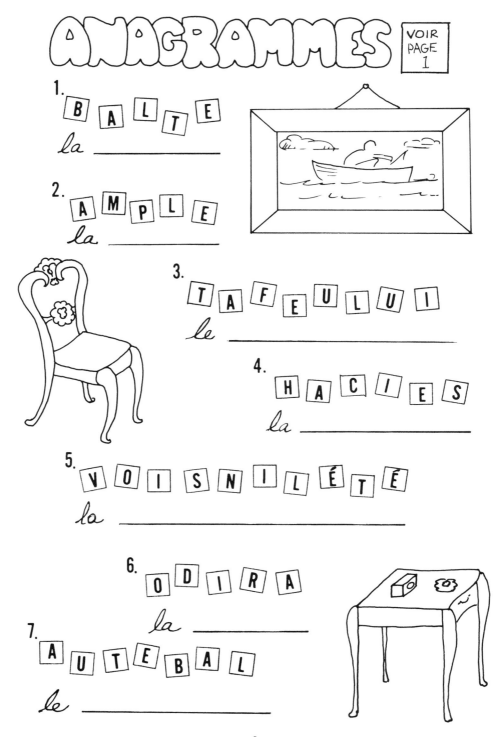

1. B A L T E

   la _____

2. A M P L E

   la _____

3. T A F E U L U I

   le _____

4. H A C I E S

   la _____

5. V O I S N I L É T É

   la _____

6. O D I R A

   la _____

7. A U T E B A L

   le _____

2

ANAGRAMMES

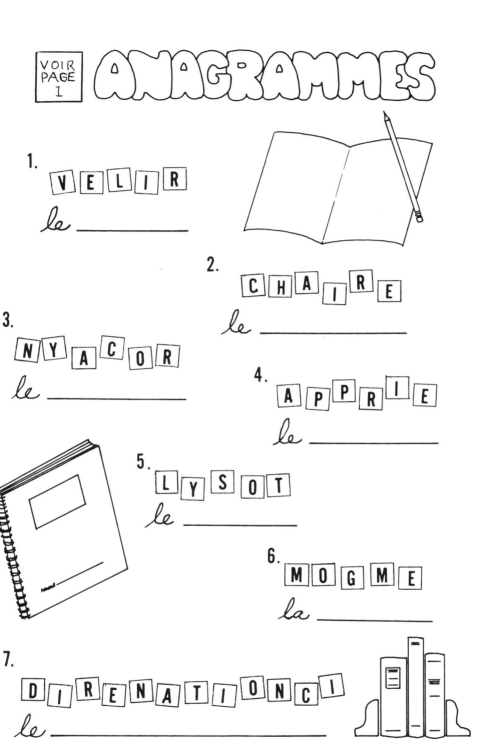

VOIR PAGE 1

1. V E L I R

le _____

2. C H A I R E

le _____

3. N Y A C O R

le _____

4. A P P R I E

le _____

5. L Y S O T

le _____

6. M O G M E

la _____

7. D I R E N A T I O N C I

le _____

ANAGRAMMES

VOIR PAGE 1

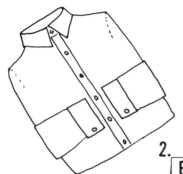

1. R O I S E U L S

les _____

2. E T A T S E C H S S U

les _____

3. M I S E C H E

la _____

4. V E T O N S

le _____

5. V A C A T E R

la _____

6. A C A U P H E

le _____

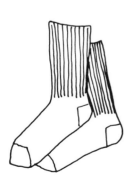

7. L A P O N T A N S

les _____

4

ANAGRAMMES

VOIR PAGE 1

1. E H R U E

l'_____

2. T U M I E N

la _____

3. É N A N E

l'_____

4. O S M I

le _____

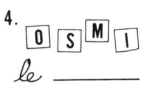

5. D O S E N C E

la _____

6. R O J U

le _____

7. M A S E I N E

la _____

ANAGRAMMES

VOIR PAGE 1

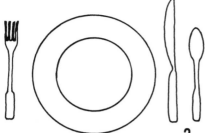

1. A S T E S

la _____

2. T R E S E T V I E

la _____

3. R E V E R

le _____

4. P A P E N

la _____

5. L I R E L U C E

la _____

6. A U T O C E U

le _____

7. T O U C H E R F E T

la _____

6

ANAGRAMMES

VOIR PAGE 1

1. P E U O S

la _____

2. O S P I N O S

le _____

3. T R E S D E S

le _____

4. T R U I F

le _____

5. D I V A N E

la _____

6. R H O S   V U E D' O R E

les _____   _____

7. M A F O R G E

le _____

7

ANAGRAMMES

VOIR PAGE 1

1. N U E L

la _____

2. L O I S E L

le _____

3. D E M O N

le _____

4. N A G E O R

l'_____

5. L E B A L

la _____

6. B O L G E

le _____

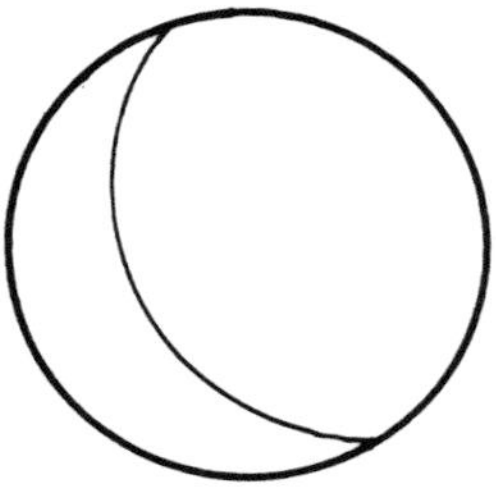

7. L O U B E   E D   G E N I E

la _____ __ _____

8

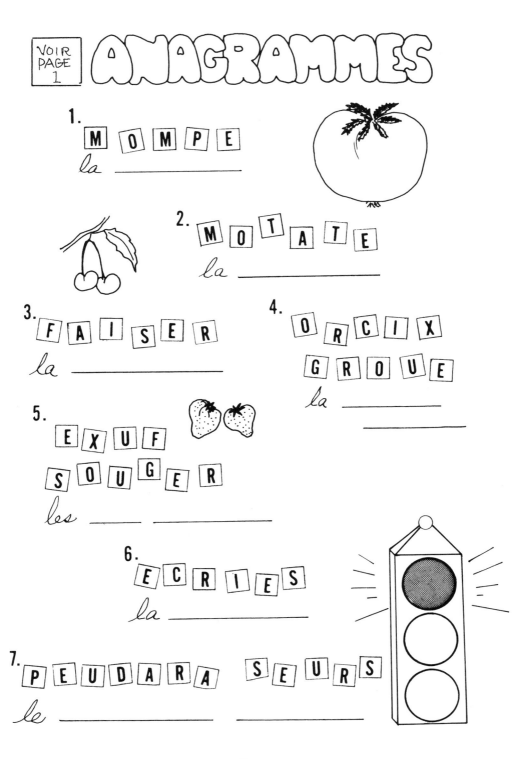

ANAGRAMMES

VOIR PAGE 1

1. M O M P E
   la _____

2. M O T A T E
   la _____

3. F A I S E R
   la _____

4. O R C I X
   G R O U E
   la _____

5. E X U F
   S O U G E R
   les ____ _____

6. E C R I E S
   la _____

7. P E U D A R A   S E U R S
   le _____   _____

9

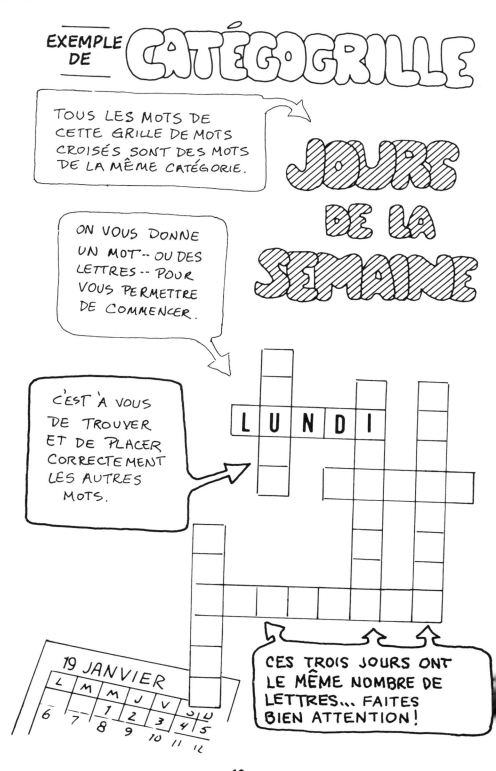

VOIR PAGE 10

CATÉGOGRILLE

NOMBRES:

1 à 10

6 ou 10?

7 ou 8?

2 ou 9?

UN

CATÉGOGRILLE

VOIR PAGE 10

NOMBRES :

11 à 20

17? 18? 19?

VOIR PAGE 10

CATÉGOGRILLE

NOMBRES

PAR DIX

13

CATÉGOGRILLE

VOIR PAGE 10

MOIS DE L'ANNÉE

FÉVRIER

1	2	3	4	5	6	7
8	9	10	11	12	13	14
15	16	17	18	19	20	21
22	23	24	25	26	27	28

J A N V I E R

14

VOIR PAGE 10

CATÉGOGRILLE

DOUZE COULEURS

| B | L | A | N | C |

CATÉGOGRILLE

VOIR PAGE 10

PRÉNOMS

(GARÇONS)

VOIR PAGE 10

CATÉGOGRILLE

PRÉNOMS

(FILLES)

| S | | M | | | | |
| | | | | | | |

| A | N | | | | | | R | | | |

| | | | | | | É | | | | B |

| | | J | | | | | | |

| L | | | | | H | |

| A | | | | A |

| G | | | | |

| Y | | | | | |

| N | | | | | |

CATÉGOGRILLE

VOIR
PAGE
10

AU
ZOO

LION

18

VOIR PAGE 10

CATÉGOGRILLE

*ATTENTION AUX PLURIELS

UN

JOYEUX

O

NOËL

É

C

MOTS DE.. NOËL

19

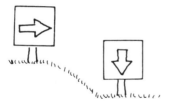

ENTRÉE

J	E	V	A	I	S	F	A	I	S
E	■	■	I	■	■	R	■	■	R
P	■	■	S	■	■	I	■	■	I
A	R	T	T	R	È	S	B	I	E
R	■	■	I	■	■	E	■	■	N
L	■	■	R	■	■	R	■	■	M
E	A	V	E	C	M	E	S	M	E
F	■	■	C	■	■	U	■	■	R
R	■	■	H	■	■	N	■	■	C
A	N	C	A	I	S	E	A	M	I

SORTIE

PHRASE LABYRINTHIQUE:

J_____I.

LABYRINTHE

VOIR PAGE 20

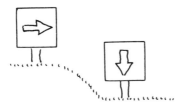
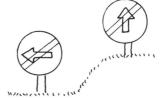

ENTRÉE →

Ⓜ	O	N	P	A	P	I	E	R	E
A	■		E	■		E	■		S
P	■		R	■		R	■		T
L	U	M	E	S	T	A	U	C	U
A	■		A	■		L	■		N
N	■		I	■		A	■		C
C	H	E	M	E	S	A	N	S	H
H	■		E	■		M	■		I
E	■		N	■		A	■		E
R	O	N	T	R	A	I	S	O	Ⓝ

SORTIE →

PHRASE LABYRINTHIQUE:

M_____N.

22

VOIR PAGE 20

LABYRINTHE

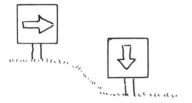 

ENTRÉE →

M	A	R	S	E	I	L	L	E	E
A			V		I		L		S
R			I		L		L		T
D	I	N	E	N	T	A	U	N	U
I			N		T		A		N
N'			T		A		V		E
E	S	U	I	T	U	N	J	O	V
S			C		T		A		I
T			I		A		T		L
P	A	S	E	N	A	V	R	I	L

→ SORTIE

PHRASE LABYRINTHIQUE:

M_____L.

23

LABYRINTHE

VOIR PAGE 20

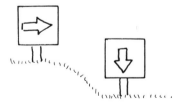

ENTRÉE →

T	R	O	I	■	S	M	O	■	I	N	S
R	■	■	S	■	■	I	■	■	■	■	U
E	■	■	E	■	■	N	■	■	■	■	N
N	■	T	E	T	R	O	S	■	M	O	I
T	■	■	T	■	■	U	■	■	■	■	S
E	■	■	R	■	■	N	■	■	■	■	T
S	A	L	O	N	S	S	■	S	U	R	D
E	■	■	I	■	■	O	■	■	■	■	E
P	■	■	S	■	■	N	■	■	■	■	U
T	O	U	■	F	O	N	T	■	S	I	X

→ SORTIE

PHRASE LABYRINTHIQUE:

T_____X.

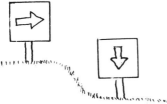

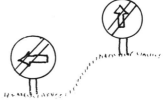

LABYRINTHE

VOIR PAGE 20

ENTRÉE

L	A	P	E	U	R	E	S	T	C
A		C			T				O
P		H			A				R
O	I	R	E	E	S	T	R	O	P
M		E			T				S
M		S			R				S
E	E	S	T	U	N	E	F	R	U
N'		B			S				I
E		R			N				T
S	T	P	A	S	N	O	I	R	E

SORTIE

PHRASE LABYRINTHIQUE :

L _____ E.

25

LABYRINTHE

VOIR PAGE 20

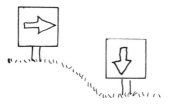

ENTRÉE →

L	E	F	R	A	N	C	A	I	S
E			A			E			E
F			S			S			S
R	È	R	E	E	S	T	U	N	P
U		E				P			O
I		S				O			I
T	E	S	T	J	O	L	I	E	S
U		S				I			S
R		E				E			O
E	N	E	S	O	N	T	B	O	N

SORTIE →

PHRASE LABYRINTHIQUE:

L_____ N .

26

VOIR PAGE 20

LABYRINTHE

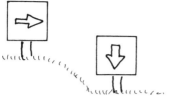

ENTRÉE

C	E	T	T	E	P	A	G	E	N'
E			E			Y			E
S			P			S			S
O	N	P	H	R	A	S	E	A	T
N			O			E			O
T			T			V			U
T	I	R	O	I	R	A	P	A	R
O			S			S			I
U			U			O			C
C	H	E	R	M	O	N	A	M	I

SORTIE

PHRASE LABYRINTHIQUE :

C_____I.

EXEMPLE DE CROIX DE MOTS

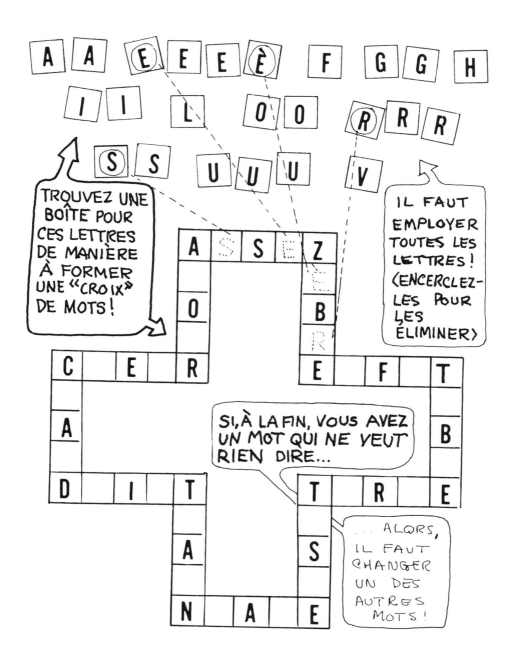

CROIX DE MOTS

VOIR PAGE 28

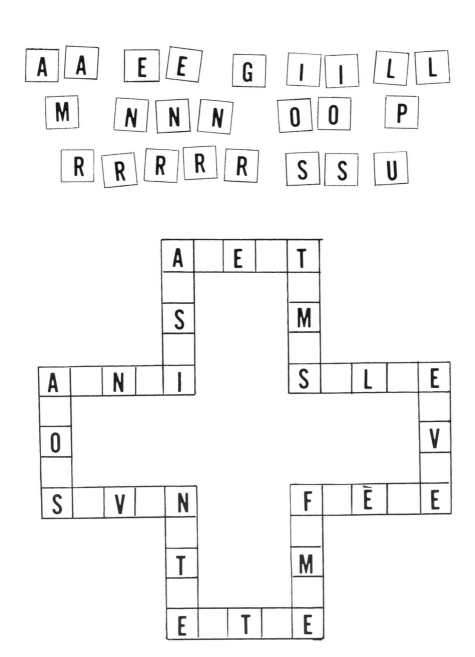

29

CROIX DE MOTS

VOIR PAGE 28

C E E G I I I L L L L

M N N R R R R R

U U V X Z

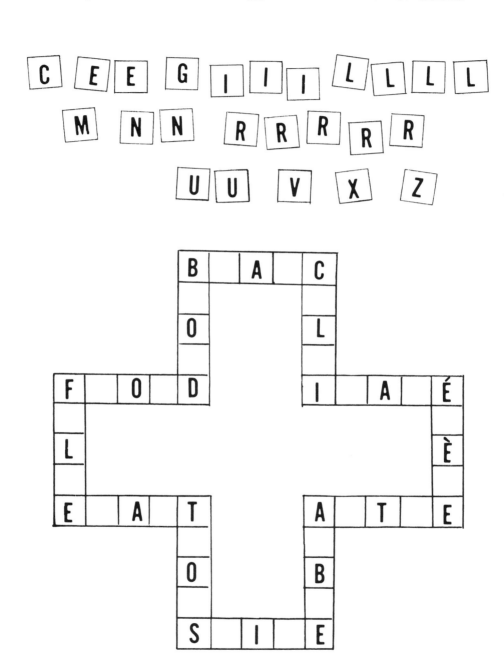

30

VOIR PAGE 28

CROIX DE MOTS

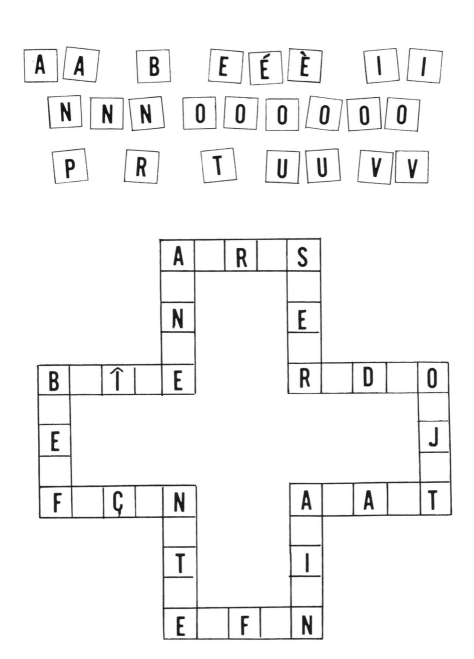

31

EXEMPLE DE MOTSTRACTIONS

> POUR RÉSOUDRE CES PROBLÈMES DE «SOUSTRACTION DE MOTS»...

> ...IL FAUT DEVINER CES DEUX MOTS-CI...

> ...ET «SOUSTRAIRE» LES LETTRES DU DEUXIÈME MOT DES LETTRES DU PREMIER

1. PAS − AS = P

2. MAISON − MOINS = A

3. 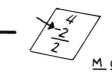 _ _ _ _ − _ _ _ = ?

4.  _ _ _ _ _ −  _ _ _ _ = ?

5. _ _ _ _ _ _ − _ _ _ _ = ?

> LES LETTRES RESTANTES VONT FORMER UN MOT QUI RÉPOND À CETTE QUESTION

QUELLE VILLE ?

MOTSTRACTIONS

VOIR PAGE 32

1.  — =

_____

2. 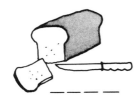 —  =

_____

3. 6 7 8 ? — =

_____

4. —  =

_____

5.  — =

_____

6.  — =

_____

QUELLES DAMES DE VOTRE FAMILLE ?

33

VOIR PAGE 32

MOTSTRACTIONS

1.

— = _ _

_ _ _ _

2.

— =

_ _

_ _ _ _ _ _ _ _

3.

— = _

_ _ _ _ _

4.

— | =

_ _ _ _ _ _ _ _

5.

— =

_ _ _ _

6. ♥ — = _

_ _ _ _ _

QUELLE VILLE ?

34

MOTSTRACTIONS

VOIR PAGE 32

1. 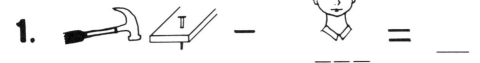 − = ___

___ ___ ___ ___ ___

2.  − = ___

___ ___ ___ ___ ___

3.  − = ___

___ ___ ___ ___ ___

4. 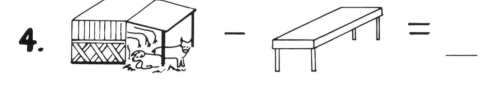 − = ___

___ ___ ___ ___ ___

5. 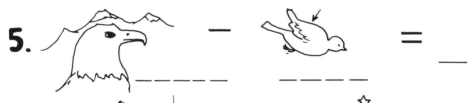 − = ___

___ ___ ___ ___ ___

6. 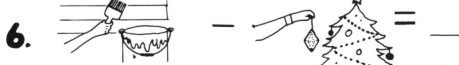 − = ___

___ ___ ___ ___ ___

QUEL BÂTIMENT ?

ARRANGEZ CES LETTRES:

___ ___ ___ ___ ___ ___

35

MOTSTRACTIONS

1.  = _ _

_ _ _ _ _ _

2. 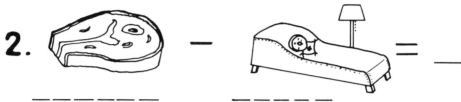 = _ _

_ _ _ _ _ _

3. 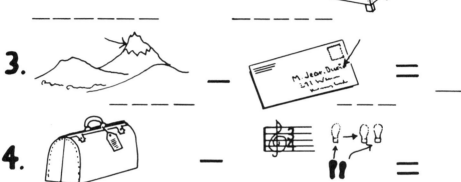 = _ _

_ _ _

4. 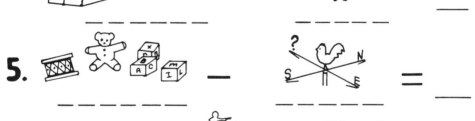 = _ _

_ _ _ _ _

5.  = _ _

_ _ _ _ _ _

6.  = _ _

_ _ _ _ _

QUEL EXPLORATEUR ?

ARRANGEZ CES LETTRES:

_ _ _ _ _ _ _

LETTRES EN CHIFFRES

D'ABORD~
REGARDEZ BIEN
LE «MOT CLEF»
ET LES
ILLUSTRATIONS
POUR DÉCOUVRIR
LA CATÉGORIE
DES MOTS À
DÉCHIFFRER~

```
1  2  3  4
N  O  I  R
```

LE MOT CLEF

```
4  2  5  6  7
R  O  U  G  E ?
```

PUIS~
INSCRIVEZ
LES LETTRES
IDENTIFIÉES
PAR LE MOT
CLEF PARTOUT
OÙ VOUS LES
VOYEZ DANS
LES AUTRES
MOTS DE LA
LISTE ~

```
2  4  8  1  6  7
O  R  _  n  _  _
```

```
4  2  9  7
R  O  _  _
```

```
6  4  3  9
_  R  i  _
```

ENFIN, EN
VOUS BASANT
SUR LES
POSITIONS
DE CES
LETTRES,
ESSAYEZ DE
DEVINER
D'AUTRES
LETTRES
ET DE
DÉCHIFFRER
TOUS LES
MOTS DE
CE GROUPE

```
10  4  5  1
 _  R  _  n
```

```
11  8  5  1  7
 _  _  _  n  _
```

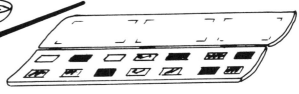

37

VOIR
PAGE
37

LETTRES EN CHIFFRES

1.
1 2 3 4
N U I T

2.
5 3 1 2 3 4
_ _ _ _ _ _

3.
5 6 4 3 1
_ _ _ _ _

4.
5 3 7 3
_ _ _ _

5.
6 8 9 10 11   5 3 7 3
_ _ _ _ _ _ _ _ _ _

6.
11 12 3 9
_ _ _ _

7.
6 2 13 10
_ _ _ _

LETTRES EN CHIFFRES

VOIR PAGE 37

1.
```
1 2 3 4
A U T O
```

2.
```
5 1 3 6 1 2
_ _ _ _ _ _
```

3.
```
3 7 1 8 9
_ _ _ _ _
```

4.
```
1 10 8 4 9
_ _ _ _ _
```

5.
```
1 2 3 4 5 2 11
_ _ _ _ _ _ _
```

6.
```
1 2 3 4 12 17
_ _ _ _ _ _
```

7.
```
3 1 13 8
_ _ _ _
```

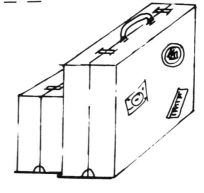

39

VOIR
PAGE
37

LETTRES EN CHIFFRES

1.
1 2 3 4
R O B E

2.
3 5 6
_ _ _

3.
3 7 2 8 6 4
_ _ _ _ _ _

4.
6 2 8 7 9 4 1 6
_ _ _ _ _ _ _ _

5.
10 8 11 4
_ _ _ _

6.
12 13 5 11 4 5 8
_ _ _ _ _ _ _

7.
4 12 13 5 1 11 4
_ _ _ _ _ _ _

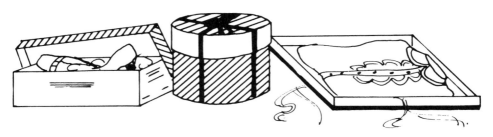

LETTRES EN CHIFFRES

VOIR PAGE 37

1.
1 2 3 4
C H A T
‾ ‾ ‾ ‾

2.
1 2 5 6 3 7
‾ ‾ ‾ ‾ ‾ ‾

3.
1 2 8 5 9
‾ ‾ ‾ ‾ ‾

4.
6 3 1 2 5
‾ ‾ ‾ ‾ ‾

5.
1 2 5 6 10 5
‾ ‾ ‾ ‾ ‾ ‾

6.
1 11 1 2 11 9
‾ ‾ ‾ ‾ ‾ ‾

7.
12 11 13 4 11 9
‾ ‾ ‾ ‾ ‾ ‾

41

VOIR PAGE 37

LETTRES EN CHIFFRES

1.
1 2 3 4
C A F É

2.
1 5 1 2 1 5 6 2
_ _ _ _ _ _ _ _

3.
1 7 5 1 5 6 2 8
_ _ _ _ _ _ _ _

4.
6 2 9 8
_ _ _ _

5.
8 7 4
_ _ _'

6.
6 9 10 5 11 2 12 4
_ _ _ _ _ _ _ _

7.
4 2 13
_ _ _

10 9 11 4 14 2 6 4
_ _ _ _ _ _ _ _

LETTRES EN CHIFFRES

VOIR PAGE 37

1.
$\underset{C}{1}\ \underset{O}{2}\ \underset{U}{3}$

2.
$\underset{\_}{1}\ \underset{\_}{2}\ \underset{\_}{3}\ \underset{\_}{4}\ \underset{\_}{5}$

3.
$\underset{\_}{6}\ \underset{\_}{5}\ \underset{\_}{7}\ \underset{\_}{2}\ \underset{\_}{3}$

4.
$\underset{\_}{8}\ \underset{\_}{9}\ \underset{\_}{5}\ \underset{\_}{4}$

5.
$\underset{\_}{4}\ \underset{\_}{2}\ \underset{\_}{9}\ \underset{\_}{6}\ \underset{\_}{10}$

6.
$\underset{\_}{10}\ \underset{\widehat{\_}}{5}\ \underset{\_}{10}\ \underset{\_}{5}$

7.
$\underset{\_}{8}\ \underset{\_}{2}\ \underset{\_}{3}\ \underset{\_}{1}\ \underset{\_}{5}$

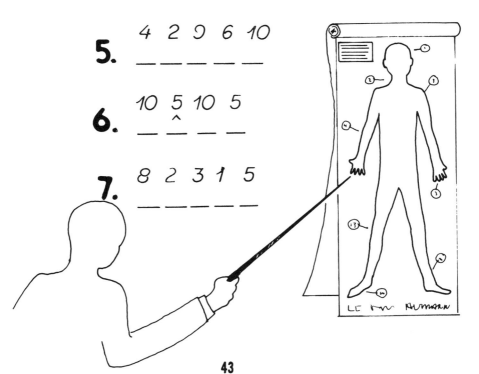

LE CORPS HUMAIN

43

VOIR PAGE 37

LETTRES EN CHIFFRES

1.
1 2 3 2 4 2
C A N A D A

2.
5 6 2 3 1 9
_ _ _ _ _ _

3.
2 3 7 8 9 10 9 6 6 9
_ _ _ _ _ _ _ _ _ _

4.
2 6 7 9 3 10 11 3 9
_ _ _ _ _ _ _ _ _

5.
2 8 8 9 12 2 7 3 9
_ _ _ _ _ _ _ _ _

6.
11 6 8 2 3 4 9
_ _ _ _ _ _ _

7.
11 3 4 9
_ _ _ _

LETTRES EN CHIFFRES

VOIR PAGE 37

1. 1 2 3 4
‗ ‗ ‗ —

2. 1 2 3 3 5
‗ ‗ ‗ ‗ —

3. 1 6 5 6 5
‗ ‗ ‗ ‗ —

4. 7 5 6 5
‗ ‗ ‗ —

5. 8 5 6 5
‗ ‗ ‗ —

6. 4 9 5 10 6
‗ ‗ ‗ ‗ —

7. 1 11 8 2 3 3 5
‗ ‗ ‗ ‗ ‗ ‗ —

VOIR PAGE 37

LETTRES EN CHIFFRES

1. _1 2 3_
___ ___ ___

2. _1 2 4 5_
___ ___ ___ ___

3. _2 6 4 3 7_
___ ___ ___ ___ ___

4. _8 2 9 6 3 10 4_
___ ___ ___ ___ ___ ___ ___

5. _8 11 3 9_
___ ___ ___ ___

6. _8 11 3 7 7 10 12_
___ ___ ___ ___ ___ ___ ___

7. _2 13 11 12_
___ ___ ___ ___

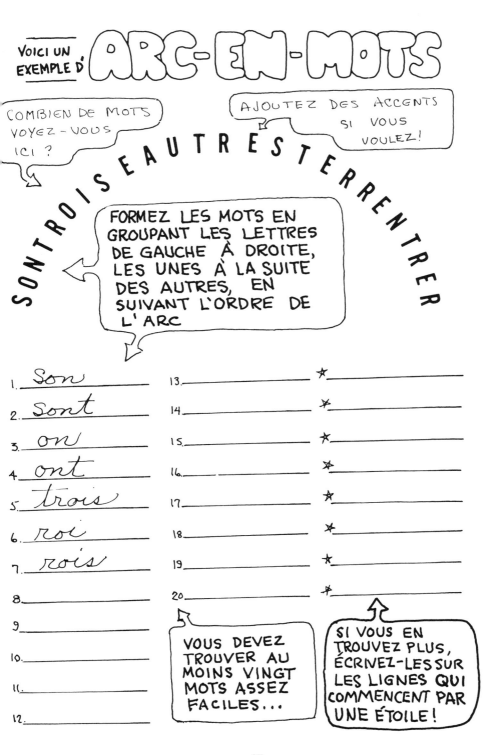

VOICI UN EXEMPLE D' ARC-EN-MOTS

COMBIEN DE MOTS VOYEZ-VOUS ICI ?

AJOUTEZ DES ACCENTS SI VOUS VOULEZ!

SONTROISEAUTRESTERRENTRER

FORMEZ LES MOTS EN GROUPANT LES LETTRES DE GAUCHE À DROITE, LES UNES À LA SUITE DES AUTRES, EN SUIVANT L'ORDRE DE L'ARC

1. Son
2. Sont
3. on
4. ont
5. trois
6. roi
7. rois
8. ___
9. ___
10. ___
11. ___
12. ___

13. ___
14. ___
15. ___
16. ___
17. ___
18. ___
19. ___
20. ___

* ___
* ___
* ___
* ___
* ___
* ___
* ___
* ___

VOUS DEVEZ TROUVER AU MOINS VINGT MOTS ASSEZ FACILES...

SI VOUS EN TROUVEZ PLUS, ÉCRIVEZ-LES SUR LES LIGNES QUI COMMENCENT PAR UNE ÉTOILE!

47

VOIR PAGE 47

ARC-EN-MOTS

BOUCHERIENFINIMAGENOUVEAUX

20 MOTS OU PLUS?

1. _____

2. _____

3. _____

4. _____

5. _____

6. _____

7. _____

8. _____

9. _____

10. _____

11. _____

12. _____

13. _____

14. _____

15. _____

16. _____

17. _____

18. _____

19. _____

20. _____

☆ _____

☆ _____

☆ _____

☆ _____

☆ _____

☆ _____

☆ _____

☆ _____

☆ _____

_____

_____

_____

48

ARC-EN-MOTS

VOIR PAGE 47

ATTENTION AUX ACCENTS!

D E D A N S A V O I R A M E N E T E

20 MOTS OU PLUS?

1. _____
2. _____
3. _____
4. _____
5. _____
6. _____
7. _____
8. _____
9. _____
10. _____
11. _____
12. _____

13. _____
14. _____
15. _____
16. _____
17. _____
18. _____
19. _____
20. _____
✷ _____
✷ _____
✷ _____
✷ _____

✷ _____
✷ _____
✷ _____
✷ _____
✷ _____
_____
_____
_____
_____
_____
_____
_____

49

VOIR PAGE 47

ARC-EN-MOTS

ARBREVENIRADISCOURSEMAINEZERO

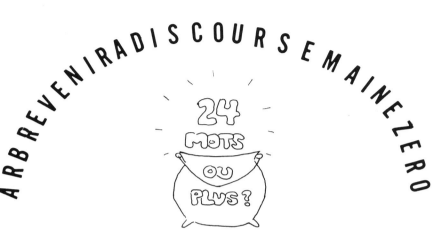

24 MOTS OU PLUS?

1. _____
2. _____
3. _____
4. _____
5. _____
6. _____
7. _____
8. _____
9. _____
10. _____
11. _____
12. _____

13. _____
14. _____
15. _____
16. _____
17. _____
18. _____
19. _____
20. _____
21. _____
22. _____
23. _____
24. _____

★_____
★_____
★_____
★_____
★_____
★_____
★_____
★_____
_____
_____
_____

50

ARC-EN-MOTS

VOIR PAGE 47

MAISONNETTESSENCELARGENTILECONTELLE

24 MOTS OU PLUS ?

1. _____
2. _____
3. _____
4. _____
5. _____
6. _____
7. _____
8. _____
9. _____
10. _____
11. _____
12. _____

13. _____
14. _____
15. _____
16. _____
17. _____
18. _____
19. _____
20. _____
21. _____
22. _____
23. _____
24. _____

★ _____
★ _____
★ _____
★ _____
★ _____
★ _____
_____
_____
_____
_____
_____
_____

VOIR PAGE 47

ARC-EN-MOTS

VERSOIFAIMERCINEMALADEJEUNERVEUX

24 MOTS OU PLUS?

1. _____
2. _____
3. _____
4. _____
5. _____
6. _____
7. _____
8. _____
9. _____
10. _____
11. _____
12. _____

13. _____
14. _____
15. _____
16. _____
17. _____
18. _____
19. _____
20. _____
21. _____
22. _____
23. _____
24. _____

★ _____
★ _____
★ _____
★ _____
★ _____
★ _____
★ _____
★ _____
★ _____
★ _____
★ _____
★ _____

ARC-EN-MOTS

VOIR PAGE 47

FAMILLE SURPRISE LE VERTÉTES

30 MOTS OU PLUS ?

1. _____

2. _____

3. _____

4. _____

5. _____

6. _____

7. _____

8. _____

9. _____

10. _____

11. _____

12. _____

13. _____

14. _____

15. _____

16. _____

17. _____

18. _____

19. _____

20. _____

21. _____

22. _____

23. _____

24. _____

25. _____

26. _____

27. _____

28. _____

29. _____

30. _____

★ _____

★ _____

★ _____

★ _____

★ _____

★ _____

ANSWER KEY

ANAGRAMMES .... Page 9

1. POMME   (CHOSES
2. TOMATE   ROUGES)
3. FRAISE
4. CROIX ROUGE
5. FEUX ROUGES
6. CERISE
7. DRAPEAU RUSSE

CATÉGOGRILLE .... Page 10

```
J                    (JOURS)
E       D    V
L U N D I    E
  D     M    N
  I   M A R D I
      N      R
S     C      E
A     H      D
M E R C R E D I
E
D
I
```

CATÉGOGRILLE .... Page 11

```
    D              (NOMBRES:
  C I N Q           1 - 10)
    X   U N
        A
H U I   T
        R
    S E P T
N   I     R
D E U X   O
    U     I
    F     S
```

CATÉGOGRILLE .... Page 12

```
          Q        (NOMBRES:
  D I X - H U I T   11 - 20)
  O       A
  U       T
O N Z E   O
  E     T R E I Z E
          Z
  D I X - S E P T
          E
      Q U I N Z E
  V       Z
  D I X - N E U F
  N
  G
  T
```

CATÉGOGRILLE .... Page 13

```
(NOMBRES:                        S
 PAR DIX)                 T      O
               V          R      I
     S O I X A N T E - D  I      X
               N          N      A
               G          T      N
C I N Q U A N T E         E      T
     U                           E
     Q U A T R E - V I N G T S
     R
     A            C
     N            E         D
     Q U A T R E - V I N G T - D I X
     E            T         X
```

CATÉGOGRILLE .... Page 14

```
              A          (MOIS)
              V    A
J A N V I E R      O
              I    Û
      J U I L L E T
      U
M A I              S
A   N O V E M B R E
R                  P
S     F            T
      D É C E M B R E
      V            M
      R   O C T O B R E
      I            R
      E            E
      R
```

CATÉGOGRILLE .... Page 15

```
  B L A N C   B      (COULEURS)
  L       O   E
  E       I   I
B R U N   R O U G E
  O       R   E
  S       A
V E R T   N
I             G R I S
O   J A U N E
L
E
T
```

55

CATÉGOGRILLE .... Page 16

```
            F          (PRÉNOMS:
        H E N R I       GARÇONS)
            A
        J E A N   P
            A   Ç   H
            C   L O U I S
            Q   I   L
            U   S   I
M A R C E L       P
        A   S       P       R
        O           P I E R R E
    G U Y               N
        L           A N D R É
                    R
    G U I L L A U M E
                    A
                    N
        É D O U A R D
```

CATÉGOGRILLE .... Page 17

```
        S I M O N E      (PRÉNOMS:
        A                 FILLES)
        R         R
A N T O I N E T T E
    I       E       N       B
    C               É L I S E
    O       J       E       R
    L U C I E           H   T
    E       A           E   H
        A   N           A N N E
        D   N           R
G I S È L E             I
        L       Y V E T T E
        E       V       T
                O       T
                N A D I N E
                N
                E
```

CATÉGOGRILLE .... Page 18

```
        É          Z   (AU ZOO)
        L I O N    È
        É   U      B       H
L O U P     R      R       I
É   H   S I N G E          P
O   A              S       P
P   N       S              O
A   T I G R E      J       O
R       I   R      A       T
D       R   P      G       A
    C H A M E A U          M
            F   N   A      M
            E   T   R E N N E
```

CATÉGOGRILLE .... Page 19

```
            U        (MOTS
        A N G E      DE NOËL)

            J
        C L O C H E
            Y
    A R B R E
            U
C A D E A U X   J O U E T S
                R
        B O N B O N S
            O       E
            Ë       M
        É G L I S E
            T       N
C H A N S O N S     T
            I       S
            L
    C A R T E S
```

LABYRINTHE .... Page 20

```
        L
        E
        C
    H E V A
        L
        L E
        S T U N A N I
                    M
                    A
                    L
```
Le cheval est un animal.

LABYRINTHE .... Page 21

```
    J E V A
        I
        S
    T R È S B I E
                N
                M
                E
                R
                C
                I
```
Je vais très bien, merci.

LABYRINTHE . . . . **Page 22**

```
M O N P
      È
      R
      E
      A
      I
    M E S A
          M
          A
        I S O N
```

Mon père aime sa maison.

LABYRINTHE . . . . **Page 23**

```
M A R S
      V
      I
    E N T A
        V
        A
        N
        T
        A
      V R I L
```

Mars vient avant avril.

LABYRINTHE . . . . **Page 24**

```
T R O I
      S
      E
      T
      T
      R
      O
      I
      S
    F O N T S I X
```

Trois et trois font six.

LABYRINTHE . . . . **Page 25**

```
L
A
P
O
M
M
E
N'
E
S T P A S N O I R E
```

La pomme n'est pas noire.

LABYRINTHE . . . . **Page 26**

```
L
E
F
R
U
I
  T E S T J O L
              I
              E
            T B O N
```

Le fruit est joli et bon.

LABYRINTHE . . . . **Page 27**

```
C E T T
      E
      P
    H R A S
          E
          V
        A P A R
              I
              C
              I
```

Cette phrase va par ici.

CROIX DE MOTS . . . . **Page 28**

```
        A S S E Z
        V       È
        O       B
        I       R
  C O E U R   E F F E T
  H                   A
  A                   B
  U                   L
  D O I G T   T E R R E
        R     A
        A     S
        I     S
        N U A G E
```

CROIX DE MOTS . . . . **Page 29**

```
        A G E N T
        U     E
        S     M
        S     P
  A I N S I   S A L L E
  L                   N
  O                   V
  R                   I
  S A V O N   F R È R E
        O     E
        T     M
        R     M
        E N T R E
```

57

CROIX DE MOTS .... **Page 30**

```
      B L A N C
      L       E
      O       L
      N       U
  F R O I D      I M A G É
  I               L
  L               È
  L               V
  E X A C T     A U T R E
      R         R
      O         B
      I         R
      S E I Z E
```

CROIX DE MOTS .... **Page 31**

```
      A P R È S
      N       O
      N       E
      É       U
  B O Î T E     R A D I O
  O             B
  E             J
  U             E
  F A Ç O N     A V A N T
      O       V
      T       I
      R       O
      E N F I N
```

MOTSTRACTIONS .... **Page 32**

PAS – AS = P
MAISON – MOINS = A
BRAS – BAS = R
SINGE – GENS = I
BROSSE – ROBES = S

   VILLE: PARIS

MOTSTRACTIONS .... **Page 33**

BALLET – BALLE = T
PAIN – PIN = A
NEUF – FEU = N
TROIS – ROIS = T
QUATRE – QUART = E
POISSON – POISON = S

   DAMES: TANTES

MOTSTRACTIONS .... **Page 34**

PAQUET – TAUPE = Q
NUAGE – ANGE = U
GÉANT – GANT = É

BOEUF – OEUF = B
POUCE – COUP = E
COEUR – ROUE = C

   VILLE: QUÉBEC

MOTSTRACTIONS .... **Page 35**

CLOU – COU = L
POULE – LOUP = E
BOÎTES – BOÎTE = S
ÉTABLE – TABLE = É
AIGLE – AILE = G
PEINDRE – PENDRE = I

   BÂTIMENT: ÉGLISE

MOTSTRACTIONS .... **Page 36**

BLANC – BANC = L
VIANDE – DIVAN = E
MONT – NOM = T
VALISE – VALSE = I
JOUETS – OUEST = J
COURSE – SUCRE = O

   EXPLORATEUR: JOLIET

CHIFFRES .... **Page 37**

1. NOIR   (COULEURS)
2. ROUGE
3. ORANGE
4. ROSE
5. GRIS
6. BRUN
7. JAUNE

CHIFFRES .... **Page 38**

1. NUIT   (MOMENTS DE
2. MINUIT   LA JOURNÉE)
3. MATIN
4. MIDI
5. APRÈS-MIDI
6. SOIR
7. AUBE

CHIFFRES .... **Page 39**

1. AUTO   (VOYAGE)
2. BATEAU
3. TRAIN
4. AVION
5. AUTOBUS
6. AUTOCAR
7. TAXI

CHIFFRES .... Page 40

1. ROBE (VÊTEMENTS
2. BAS FÉMININS)
3. BLOUSE
4. SOULIERS
5. JUPE
6. CHAPEAU
7. ÉCHARPE

CHIFFRES .... Page 41

1. CHAT (ANIMAUX)
2. CHEVAL
3. CHIEN
4. VACHE
5. CHÈVRE
6. COCHON
7. MOUTON

CHIFFRES .... Page 42

1. CAFÉ (BOISSONS)
2. COCA COLA
3. CHOCOLAT
4. LAIT
5. THÉ
6. LIMONADE
7. EAU MINÉRALE

CHIFFRES .... Page 43

1. COU (PARTIES
2. COUDE DU CORPS)
3. GENOU
4. PIED
5. DOIGT
6. TÊTE
7. POUCE

CHIFFRES .... Page 44

1. CANADA (PAYS)
2. FRANCE
3. ANGLETERRE
4. ARGENTINE
5. ALLEMAGNE
6. IRLANDE
7. INDE

CHIFFRES .... Page 45

1. FILS (FAMILLE)
2. FILLE
3. FRÈRE
4. PÈRE
5. MÈRE
6. SOEUR
7. FAMILLE

CHIFFRES .... Page 46

1. MAI (MOIS)
2. MARS
3. AVRIL
4. JANVIER
5. JUIN
6. JUILLET
7. AOÛT

ARC-EN-MOTS .... Page 47

SON	OISEAU	TRÈS
SONT	SE	RESTE
ON	SEAU	RESTÉ
ONT	EAU	RESTER
TROIS	AU	ES
ROI	AUTRE	EST
ROIS	AUTRES	(ESTER)
TE	ERRÉ	EN
TERRE	ERRENT	ENTRE
(TERRÉ)	RENTRE	ENTRÉ
(TERRENT)	RENTRÉ	ENTRER
ERRE	RENTRER	(RE)

ARC-EN-MOTS .... Page 48

BOUC	RI	GENOU
BOUCHE	RIEN	NOUVEAU
(BOUCHÉ)	EN	NOUVEAUX
BOUCHER	ENFIN	VEAU
BOUCHERIE	FIN	VEAUX
OU	FINI	EAU
OÙ	IMAGE	EAUX
CHER	MA	AU
CHÉRI	(MAGE)	AUX
CHÉRIE	ÂGE	

ARC-EN-MOTS .... Page 49

DE	VOIR	MÈNE
DÉ	IRA	MENÉ
DEDANS	(RAME)	EN
DANS	(RAMÉ)	NE
(DANSA)	RAMÈNE	NÉ
AN	RAMENÉ	NET
ANS	ÂME	ET
SA	AMÈNE	ÉTÉ
SAVOIR	AMENÉ	TE
AVOIR	ME	

ARC-EN-MOTS . . . . Page 50

ARBRE	COU	MA
BRÈVE	COUR	MAI
RÊVE	COURS	MAIN
RÊVÉ	COURSE	MAINE
EVE	OU	AÎNÉ
VENIR	OÙ	AI
EN	OURS	NE
NI	OURSE	NÉ
RADIS	SE	NEZ
DIS	(SEMA)	ZÉRO
DISCOURS	SEMAINE	

ARC-EN-MOTS . . . . Page 51

MA	NETTE	EN
MAI	NETTES	IL
MAIS	ET	ÎLE
MAISON	TE	LE
MAISON-	TES	LECON
NETTE	ES	CONTE
AI	ESSENCE	CONTÉ
SON	EN	ON
SONNE	CE	ONT
SONNÉ	CELA	TE
SONNET	LA	TEL
SONNETTE	LÀ	TELLE
ON	LARGE	ELLE
NE	ARGENT	LE
NÉ	GENT	
NET	GENTIL	

ARC-EN-MOTS . . . . Page 52

VER	CI	DÉJEUNÉ
VERS	CINÉ	DÉJEUNER
VERSO	CINÉMA	JE
SOI	NE	JEU
SOIF	NÉ	JEUNE
FAIM	MA	EU
AI	MAL	UN
AIME	MALADE	UNE
AIMÉ	LA	NE
AIMER	LÀ	NÉ
ME	DE	NERVEUX
MER	DÉ	VEUX
MERCI	DÉJEUNE	EUX

ARC-EN-MOTS . . . . Page 53

FAMILLE	SURPRISE	VER
AMI	PRIS	VERT
(MI)	PRISE	VERTE
MIL	RIS	TE
MILLE	SE	TÊTE
IL	SEL	TÊTES
LE	ÉLÈVE	ET
LES	ÉLEVÉ	ÉTÉ
ES	ÉLEVER	ÊTES
SU	LÈVE	TES
SUR	LEVÉ	ES
SURPRIS	LEVER	